THE
BYZANTINE
EMPIRE

For my parents, Everett and Harriet Marston

With thanks to Dr. Martha P. Vinson,
Associate Professor of Byzantine Studies at Indiana University,
for her thoughtful reading of the manuscript

CULTURES
OF THE PAST

THE
BYZANTINE
EMPIRE

ELSA MARSTON

BENCHMARK BOOKS

MARSHALL CAVENDISH
NEW YORK

Benchmark Books
Marshall Cavendish
99 White Plains Road
Tarrytown, New York 10591-9001
www.marshallcavendish.com

Library of Congress Cataloging-in-Publication Data

Marston, Elsa.
    The Byzantine Empire / by Elsa Marston.
        p.   cm. — (Cultures of the past)
    Summary: Describes the culture and traces the history and lasting influences
of the Byzantine Empire, which grew from the decaying Roman empire and ruled
from Constantinople from the fourth to the fifteenth century.
    Includes bibliographical references and index.
    ISBN 0-7614-1495-9
    1. Byzantine Empire—History—Juvenile literature. [1. Byzantine Empire—
History.] I. Title. II. Series.
DF552 .M37   2003
949.5'02—dc21   2002003222

Printed in Hong Kong
1 3 5 6 4 2

Book design by Carol Matsuyama
Art research by Rose Corbett Gordon, Mystic CT.

Front cover: A mosaic of Emperor Constantine IX
Back cover: A fifth-century mosaic from Ravenna, Italy

Photo Credits

Front cover: Robert Frerck/Woodfin Camp & Associates; back cover: The Granger
Collection, New York; page 7: Stapleton Collection/Bridgeman Art Library; pages 8,
20, 32–33, 53: Erich Lessing/Art Resource, NY; page 11: Adam Woolfitt/Woodfin
Camp & Associates; pages 13, 57: San Vitale, Ravenna, Italy/Bridgeman Art Library;
pages 17, 46, 48: Werner Forman/Art Resource, NY; page 22: Palazzo Ducale, Venice/
Bridgeman Art Library; page 24: Musée des Augustins, Toulouse, France/Bridgeman
Art Library; pages 27, 31, 63: Scala/Art Resource, NY; pages 29: Alinari/Art Resource,
NY; page 35: Giraudon/Art Resource, NY; page 39: Biblioteca Apostolica Vaticana
Barb.GR.372 F.43v; pages 44: Bibliotheque Nationale, Paris/Bridgeman Art Library;
pages: 47, 50–51: Robert Frerck/Woodfin Camp & Associates; 52, 54, 72–73: The
Granger Collection, New York; pages 58, 71: Lindsay Hebberd/Woodfin Camp &
Associates; page 60: San Apollonia, Ravenna, Italy/Bridgeman Art Library; page 62:
Monastery of Saint Catherine, Mount Sinai, Egypt/Ancient Art and Architecture
Collection Ltd/Bridgeman Art Library; page 65: Cameraphoto/Art Resource, NY;
page 66: Wally McNamee/Woodfin Camp & Associates; page 67: Geoffrey Clifford/
Woodfin Camp & Associates; page 69: Wallraf-Richartz Museum, Cologne/
Bridgeman Art Library

CONTENTS

CHAPTER ONE

THE EMPIRE OF THE EAST

Wearing his imperial armor, Emperor Constantine XI paced the ramparts of the city walls on a warm spring night, May 28, 1453. Those walls had kept invaders out of Constantinople for hundreds of years, but Constantine knew they could not hold much longer. Gazing out into the darkness, he could see a semicircle of twinkling lights—the enemy's lanterns, too numerous to count.

His men, less than seven thousand against an army many times larger, looked to Constantine for courage. As he contemplated what lay ahead, he thought of the long story of the empire he still commanded. And he knew that he would fight to the very end.

A scene much like this probably took place on the eve of a major turning point in history. Eleven hundred years had led up to the crisis faced by the eleventh emperor to bear the illustrious name of Constantine. Now let us go back to the beginning.

From Rome to Byzantium

What we call the Byzantine (BIH-zen-teen) Empire was, in fact, a direct continuation of the Roman Empire. For centuries, from the city of Rome in Italy, the Romans had governed an enormous territory that included Europe, North Africa, and western Asia. By the middle of the third century C.E.*, however, Rome's glory days were over. In Europe, Germanic tribes were pounding at its borders, while in Syria and Egypt, rebels boldly defied their Roman rulers. Chaos and corruption reigned in Rome itself,

*Many systems of dating have been used by different cultures throughout history. This series of books uses B.C.E. (Before Common Era) and C.E. (Common Era) instead of B.C. (Before Christ) and A.D. (Anno Domini) out of respect for the diversity of the world's peoples.

A fifteenth-century German artist created this wood-block print of Constantinople, showing the city's watery setting, formidable walls, and hilly terrain.

where emperors were changed frequently at the whim of military leaders.

Finally, in 284, a strong emperor named Diocletian managed to take power. Diocletian decided to avoid Rome and live instead in a city in western Anatolia (now Turkey). To improve the way the empire was ruled, he decreed that there should be *two* emperors. One would rule the western part—Italy, western Europe, Britain, and North Africa. The other would command the eastern part— the Balkans, Anatolia, Syria, Palestine, and Egypt. Each emperor would have a second-in-command, making a total of four corulers.

In 305 Diocletian voluntarily retired. His new arrangement for an orderly system of succession did not last long, however. When the western emperor died in Britain in 306, the military troops there acclaimed his son as the successor. That young man, named Constantine (KON-stan-teen), was destined to change the course of world history. Over the next eighteen years Constantine managed to eliminate the other three corulers in battle, and by 324 he was the sole emperor of the Roman Empire.

Constantine I holds a model of the great city he established as the seat of his empire.

The New Capital

Like Diocletian, Constantine chose to live in an eastern city rather than in Rome. He decided that the empire should have a new capital, one that was appropriate for a glorious new future. The eastern provinces, where a strong Greek culture overlay the heritage of many ancient civilizations, were rich in both population and resources. Moreover, Constantine had become deeply involved with the growing religion of Christianity, which had its roots in the East.

The site Constantine chose for his new capital was a town called Byzantium (bih-ZAN-tee-um). It had been founded as a Greek trading colony about a thousand years earlier. Although not a famous or powerful city, Byzantium had been fought over many times because of its strategic location, which was important for both the city's prosperity and its defense.

Byzantium stood partway along the straits between the Aegean Sea (east of Greece) and the Black Sea. It occupied the tip of a small peninsula, with a body of water to the south called the Sea of Marmara, which led to a passage called the Bosporus. One side of the peninsula was formed by a narrow inlet, known as the Golden Horn because its shape resembled the horn of a stag. The Golden Horn, deep and protected, provided an excellent harbor for ships.

Having decided on Byzantium as his capital, Constantine changed its name to Constantinople. He promptly set to work building a magnificent city. A new population of Roman aristocrats was encouraged to come and settle in the new capital. In the year 330 Constantine—known in history as Constantine I or Constantine the Great—formally inaugurated his city as the seat of the revitalized Roman Empire. That date is generally considered the beginning of Byzantine history.

We call the territory ruled from Constantinople the Byzantine Empire, and we often refer to the empire's government and culture simply as Byzantium. Those are the terms used in this book. But the people of that empire looked at themselves differently. Throughout their empire's history they regarded it as the *Roman* Empire and called themselves Romans—even though their language and culture were Greek! This confusion in terms has to be kept in mind when reading Byzantine history, for when Byzantine writers mentioned the "Romans," they really meant what we call the Byzantines.

Growth and Loss

Constantinople grew rapidly. A hundred years after its founding, new walls had to be constructed far beyond the earlier limits of Constantine's city. The double walls and moat built by Emperor Theodosius II (reigned 408–450), plus formidable walls all along the seafront, made Constantinople one of the best fortified cities in the world. The imposing walls of Theodosius still stand today.

CONSTANTINOPLE, THE GOLDEN CITY

The emperors Constantine I and Justinian I created the general plan of Constantinople, which remained basically the same until the end of the Byzantine Empire. In the twelfth century, one of its "golden ages," Constantinople was the jewel of all Christendom—perhaps of the world.

A grand colonnade ran along the main street, a triumphal route from the Golden Gate in the city walls all the way to the Great Palace. High columns with statues of Byzantine emperors on top decorated the forums, along with many statues brought from Greece and Rome. The city's water supply, which came by aqueducts from hills outside the city, was stored in immense and elegant underground cisterns. There was even a sewage system. Western Europe had nothing like that!

The largest imperial palace boasted golden throne rooms, banquet halls, private residences, and gardens. It also had churches, libraries, polo grounds, a riding school, a swimming pool, barracks . . . and dungeons.

Because of its location as a meeting place between East and West, Constantinople dominated the world market. The docks along the Golden Horn were crowded with all sorts of boats, while the streets teemed with people, including Scandinavians, Franks, Egyptians, Berbers from North Africa, and Persians. Shops displayed luxury goods such as silks, exquisite gold jewelry, ivory carvings, fine leather, perfumes, delicate glass, and ceramics.

In their heyday the Byzantines amassed enormous wealth and spent it adorning their city. Most of Constantinople was eventually covered over by the buildings of the Ottoman Turks, who captured the city in 1453, but its architecture inspired the design of several of the most beautiful Ottoman mosques.

Constantinople had several large and elegant cisterns to hold its water supply. Today visitors can walk through this one, built in the sixth century and now called the Sunken Palace.

Even as Constantinople thrived, the empire faced great dangers. Not long after Constantine's death in 337 it had been divided again, with the eastern part ruled from Constantinople and the western part from Rome. The threat of tribal peoples who had rampaged across central Europe for many years grew stronger than ever. These groups, called barbarians by the Byzantines and by many historians today, included the Huns under their leader Attila, Visigoths, Ostrogoths, Slavs, Avars, and Bulgars.

In the western Mediterranean a large group called the Vandals came down through Spain and seized the rich Roman provinces of North Africa. Finally, in 476, the city of Rome fell to the barbarians, and much of Italy came to be ruled by Germanic peoples: the Ostrogoths and later the Lombards. From then on the old Roman Empire had only one emperor and one seat—both at Constantinople.

The Age of Justinian

The sixth century brought a burst of enormous energy in the Byzantine Empire. Emperor Justinian I (reigned 527–565) stands out in history as one of the most famous of all rulers in the Mediterranean world. Determined to reclaim as much territory of the old Roman Empire as possible, he launched major campaigns in Europe and North Africa. His generals, particularly the extraordinary young Belisarius (beh-luh-SAR-ee-us), won back North Africa, southeast Spain, and Italy, until once more the Mediterranean was a "Roman lake." All the empire's frontiers in Europe were heavily fortified.

Justinian improved the way the empire was governed and left an impressive legacy in both legal reforms and splendid buildings. But in trying to restore the territory and grandeur of the Roman Empire, he attempted far too much, exhausting his resources. The decades following Justinian's rule brought drastic changes.

Embattled Empire: Persian and Arab Foes

Over the centuries the Byzantine Empire constantly had to fight off attackers from all directions. Some wanted to seize Byzantine territory and some wanted to capture Constantinople itself, with its fabulous riches and strategic location for trade.

The Byzantines loved chariot racing. Every sizable Byzantine city had a hippodrome—an oval stadium—and the one at Constantinople could seat around 60,000 people. The teams of charioteers, named after the colors they wore, were cheered on by fans as passionate as any football team has today. By the time of Justinian I, the fans had grown into two large factions: the Blues and the Greens. Intensely hostile to each other, the factions sometimes became unruly gangs.

At this time the public was growing angry over brutal and corrupt government officials. Trouble was brewing. Passions driven by rivalry between the Blues and Greens made the crowd ripe for mob hysteria.

One day in January 532, when Justinian was at the Hippodrome for the races, the crowd started shouting insults at him—and suddenly went wild. *"Nika! Nika!* (Victory!)"* they shouted, as they usually cheered on the charioteers. But now they were bent on destruction. Rushing out of the Hippodrome, the mob went on a dreadful rampage for five days, burning and destroying much of the city.

Desperate, Justinian thought of escaping. At that point his empress, the beautiful and determined Theodora, put him to shame. How, she asked, could an emperor ever become a fugitive? For herself, she favored the old saying that purple—the color of royalty—made the best shroud. She would stay and face the action, no matter what.

Emperor Justinian I with his general Belisarius and other military and religious figures. This famous mosaic, in the sixth-century church of San Vitale, at Ravenna, helped assert Justinian's claim that he had restored Byzantine control over Italy.

That stiffened Justinian's backbone. He called on his general Belisarius. Three thousand soldiers headed for the Hippodrome, where a huge crowd had gathered to acclaim a rival emperor. Blocking the exits, the soldiers went to work—and slaughtered some 30,000 people.

The so-called Nika riots and their terrible conclusion put an end to the power of the Blue and Green factions. Then Justinian, firmly in command, got to work and rebuilt his city, better than ever.

One persistent foe was the Persian Empire. In 530 Belisarius defeated the Persian army in Syria. The rivalry went back and forth, however, for another hundred years. In 627, under a strong new emperor named Heraclius (reigned 610–641), the Byzantines beat the Persians decisively. Soon afterward, the Persian Empire collapsed.

The Byzantines had no time to rejoice, because a new and formidable enemy was on the march. Beginning soon after 630, Arab armies, inspired by the recently founded religion of Islam, came sweeping out of Arabia. In 636 they destroyed the Byzantine army in southern Syria. Soon the Byzantine territories of Syria, Palestine, and Egypt, plus the old Persian Empire, were drawn into the Muslim world. Arab armies continued their conquests westward across North Africa and reached Spain in 711. Most of the old Roman Empire, which Justinian had tried so hard to restore, was now lost for good.

Originally an army of desert people, the swelling Arab forces had quickly developed into a strong naval power as well. Twice they besieged the walls of Constantinople by sea, from 674 to 678 and from 717 to 718. They were finally driven off, which brought an end to the Arab advance in Europe. The Arab Muslims continued strong in the eastern Mediterranean world, however. For long stretches of time they controlled important islands including Sicily, Malta, and Crete, raiding both shipping and coastal towns. Occasionally Byzantine emperors had peaceful relations with Islamic rulers in Syria and Baghdad, but on the whole the Muslim Arabs were among the empire's toughest adversaries.

The loss of the eastern Mediterranean lands and North Africa, with their agricultural wealth, busy ports, cultural resources, and large populations, was a severe blow to the Byzantine Empire. But the empire was now much more compact and easily defended. Rather than a "Roman" empire that tried to control huge territories, it had become a Greek empire centered in the East—although still claiming to be Roman!

Attackers from the Steppes

The Persians and Arabs were not the only forces to threaten the Byzantine Empire. Throughout Byzantine history various tribal peoples from eastern Europe and from the steppes—vast grassy plains—of Asia also kept

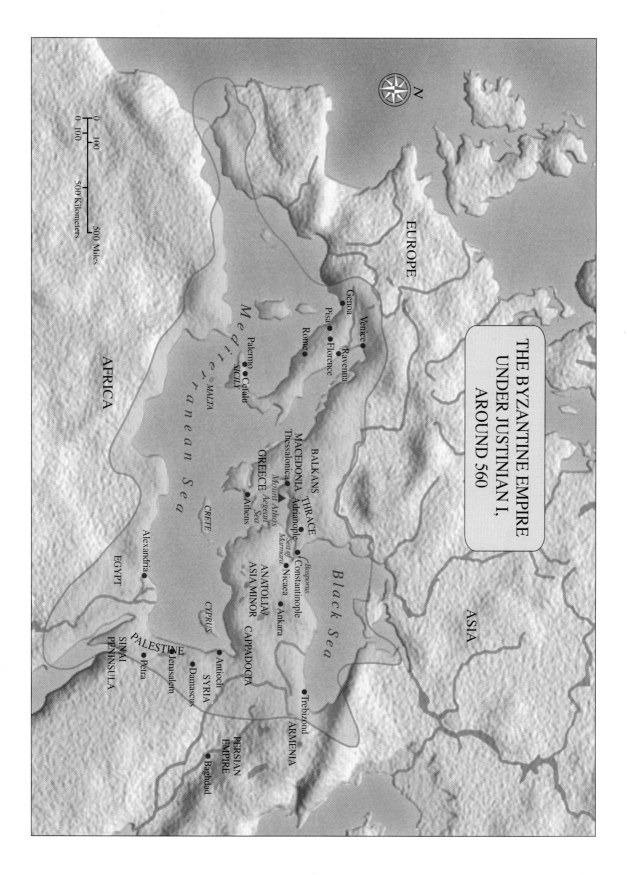

THE BYZANTINE EMPIRE
UNDER JUSTINIAN 1,
AROUND 560

N

EUROPE

AFRICA

ASIA

Venice
Genoa
Pisa
Florence
Ravenna
Rome
Palermo
Cefalù
SICILY
MALTA

Mediterranean Sea

BALKANS
MACEDONIA
Thessalonica
THRACE
Adrianople
Mount Athos
GREECE
Aegean
Sea
Athens
CRETE

Constantinople
Bosporus
Sea of
Marmara
Nicaea
Ankara
ANATOLIA/
ASIA MINOR
CAPPADOCIA

Black Sea

Trebizond
ARMENIA

Alexandria
EGYPT

CYPRUS

PALESTINE
Petra
Jerusalem
Damascus
SINAI
PENINSULA
SYRIA
Antioch

PERSIAN
EMPIRE
Baghdad

0
0
100
100
500 Kilometers
500 Miles

SOLDIERS AND FIRE

The Byzantine army was never very large—at the most probably no more than 150,000 men. But from the seventh to the twelfth centuries it was possibly the best-trained, best-equipped, best-led army in the world. It had to be—or the empire would have had a much shorter history.

Cavalrymen, highly trained and well paid, made up the army's elite troops. They were especially important on the plains of Asia, against other armies on horseback. In mountainous areas the Byzantine generals relied on their infantrymen. When besieging enemy strongholds, they used catapults, contraptions for drilling holes in walls, battering rams, and techniques for undermining the enemy's walls. The empire was also a sea power, with a navy of formidable war galleys.

Often, however, the Byzantines were on the defensive— and their most powerful weapon then was "Greek fire." This awesome substance, which ignited spontaneously, could be shot from a tube similar to a flamethrower or hurled in clay pots. Sometimes it appeared to belch from the mouths of metal lions on the prows of battleships. It clung to whatever it touched and, most terrifying of all, even burned on water.

Greek fire was invented just in time to save Constantinople from an Arab Muslim attack in 677, and it is said to have destroyed an entire Russian fleet that besieged Constantinople in 941. But exactly what was Greek fire? Perhaps a combination of sulphur, saltpeter, naphtha, liquid petroleum . . . or other mysterious ingredients? The Byzantines guarded their secret so closely that even today, scholars can only guess.

pushing toward Byzantium. From the seventh century on the most threatening were the Bulgars, who dominated the central part of the Balkans and repeatedly attacked Byzantine lands. Their power was finally broken around 1018, and their kingdom taken into the Byzantine Empire.

Russians, too, tried their luck against the empire. On three occasions they besieged Constantinople and failed. In the course of the tenth century, however, the Russian rulers were won over by Byzantine missionaries and by the splendor of the Byzantine court. The Russians converted to Christianity in 989, and in time a friendly, long-lasting alliance was formed between Russia and Byzantium.

Other pagan tribal peoples—Avars, Slavs, Magyars (Hungarians), a people called Uzes, and a tribe of fierce fighters called Pechenegs—all seized and plundered Byzantine lands in the Balkans. Sometimes the Byzantines could buy off the attackers with large amounts of gold.

This eleventh-century manuscript illustration depicts Byzantine warriors fighting off the Bulgars at Thessalonica, Greece.

Otherwise, Constantinople's famous walls and the powerful Byzantine army held them off.

The eleventh century brought two more tough rivals. The Seljuk Turks, originally from central Asia, trounced the Byzantine army in eastern Anatolia in 1071, a disastrous defeat. At the same time Norman adventurers from northern France were grabbing Byzantine territories in the Mediterranean. Under a bold and ambitious leader named Robert Guiscard (gee-SKAHR), they seized the last Byzantine outpost in Italy.

These years saw nearly constant warfare. The empire's territories sometimes shrank and sometimes expanded, depending on the abilities and determination of the emperor in power. A series of warrior-emperors in the late tenth and early eleventh centuries regained much territory in Anatolia, Armenia, and Syria, but those lands were soon lost by the weaker rulers who followed.

Then, in 1081, a capable young military officer took the throne, Alexius I of the Comnenus family. The hardworking Alexius spent most of the next thirty-seven years at war, while also carrying out important reforms in government. His son John II (reigned 1118–1143) likewise proved himself both a determined warrior and a humane ruler. The Comnenus rulers brought the empire to its last high point of strength.

Internal Weakening

Thanks to its military power, wealth, and prestige, the Byzantine Empire managed to hold its outside enemies at bay for several centuries. A bureaucracy of highly trained officials, plus the force of tradition, kept the government going through thick and thin. But a basic problem was eating away at the internal strength of the empire.

For a long time the Byzantine army had drawn its troops mainly from the rural people of Anatolia. Soldiers were rewarded for their services with permanent landholdings and provided the state with much income from taxes on their land.

By the tenth century, however, wealthy families had begun to take over the property of the small landholders. As they gained more and more land, these powerful families gave less and less support to the imperial government. Monasteries, too, were land-grabbers. The small farmers, squeezed out, could no longer provide soldiers or pay taxes as before. The army, meanwhile, had to rely increasingly on mercenary troops—hired fighters—who generally did not have the same loyalty as the native soldiers.

As the government grew poorer and weaker, conflict increased between the landed aristocracy and the central administration of the empire. During the tenth and eleventh centuries, some emperors tried to defend the common people and small landholders, while other emperors and their courts favored the wealthy families. The empire's internal structure and finances were decaying—at the very time that dangerous new enemies were appearing.

Threats from Europe: Venice and the Crusaders

By the twelfth century internal weakening and the constant threats from external foes had set the stage for disaster. The problems had begun during the reign of Alexius I. Soon after that emperor came to power in 1081, he had been forced to deal with the Norman adventurers advancing toward Constantinople. To oppose them, Alexius made an alliance with the northern Italian city of Venice, a rising commercial power. He offered large advantages in trade in return for Venice's naval support. From then on, over the next few centuries, the Venetians demanded more and more advantages, until finally Venice gained complete control of Byzantium's trade and commercial life.

Another move by Alexius produced even worse results. In 1095 the emperor asked the pope in Rome, Urban II, to send a small army to help him fight the Seljuk Turks. This simple request led to the launching of the First Crusade. Incited by the pope, masses of Europeans—including knights and common folk—undertook a march all the way across Europe and Anatolia, aiming to win back Jerusalem from the Muslims. The crusaders stopped at Constantinople on the way, then went on to Jerusalem. They took Jerusalem in 1099 and slaughtered its people: Muslims, Christians, and Jews alike.

The Byzantines had hoped that the crusaders would restore to the empire the lands they had seized in Syria and Palestine. Instead, the knights established small kingdoms for themselves in the captured lands.

The Europeans launched a second crusade in 1147 and then a third in 1189. By that time the Muslim forces, under the remarkable leader

Saladin (sah-luh-DEEN), were starting to turn back the intruders.

In 1202 the Europeans launched the Fourth Crusade, supposedly aimed at Egypt. Through a plot in which the doge (ruler) of Venice played a key role, the crusaders' army headed for Constantinople instead. This time the famous walls did not keep out the enemy. In April 1204 the crusaders took Constantinople. They destroyed much of the city, massacred great numbers of people, demolished the libraries, and looted the fabulous treasures acquired over nine centuries. It was a blow from which the Byzantines never fully recovered.

The Aftermath

Following the sack of Constantinople, Venice was given a large part of the city. The rest of the capital and other Byzantine territories were divided up into "Latin kingdoms," which were ruled by various European knights.

Of the shattered Byzantine Empire only a few small parts remained: in Anatolia and the Balkans plus the semi-independent state of Trebizond on the Black Sea. On the western coast of Anatolia a small state with the grand name of the Empire of Nicaea (nie-SEE-uh) took on the role of continuing the Byzantine Empire. Gradually this state gained more territory and power. In the 1240s it was threatened by the Seljuk Turks—and saved by a stroke of luck. Another invader from Asia, the dreaded Mongols, came sweeping into Anatolia, defeated the Turks in 1243, and then retreated. That saved the Empire of Nicaea and very probably what was left of Byzantium.

The nearly ruined Latin kingdoms run by the Europeans, meanwhile, had quickly fallen into deep economic trouble. Even Constantinople was left almost defenseless. In 1261 a small army belonging to the ambitious ruler of Nicaea, Michael VIII (reigned 1259–1282) of the Palaeologus (pay-lee-OL-oh-gus) family, took Constantinople from its discouraged Latin rulers without a fight. The Palaeologus family ruled the Byzantine Empire until its very last day.

It was hardly a secure or peaceful reign. The empire was weakened

An imaginative painting by a sixteenth-century Italian artist shows a humbled Alexius Comnenus begging the doge of Venice for military help.

The Venetians had little love for the Byzantines. In this painting by a sixteenth-century Venetian artist, the crusaders and Venetians are shown capturing Constantinople in 1204.

by the strain of trying to recover territory and by the continuing state of conflict between the landed aristocracy and the central government. Enemies threatened, including a powerful Serbian state and another dangerous European interloper named Charles of Anjou, who had made a small empire for himself in Italy and Greece. The Venetian merchants took full advantage of Byzantium's economic troubles. A Spanish mercenary army hired by the Byzantines turned against them and caused great destruction in parts of Greece under Byzantine control. The Black Death—a deadly outbreak of bubonic plague—struck in 1347, killing eight-ninths of Constantinople's population, according to one chronicler at the time. Civil wars became almost regular events.

The Last Years

In the northeastern part of Anatolia, meanwhile, another Muslim Turkish people were gaining power. These were the Ottoman Turks, named after their early leader Osman

From 1290 on the Ottomans marched relentlessly across Anatolia, until they were solidly established in the western part. From there they moved north into the Balkans, defeating the Serbs, overcoming the Hungarians, conquering the Bulgars, and taking most of Greece. By 1400 the Byzantine Empire was little more than the city of Constantinople, a fortress encircled by Turks.

What stopped the Ottomans at that point? Again the empire was saved by the actions of fierce horsemen from the steppes of Asia. The notorious Mongol conqueror Timur defeated the Ottomans at Ankara, central Anatolia, in 1402. Then, like the earlier Mongol invaders, his army mysteriously withdrew—because, it is said, Timur had decided to conquer China instead. The Ottomans' defeat, along with disunity among their leaders, gave Byzantium breathing space for another fifty years.

But the end, depicted in the opening scene of this short history, was inevitable. By the spring of 1453 the Ottomans commanded strong positions surrounding Constantinople on land and sea. They also had a determined young sultan, Mehmet II, aged twenty-one. When the Byzantines refused to surrender, Mehmet's army laid siege.

For seven weeks the far greater forces of the Turks bombarded the walls by day, employing a newly invented weapon that used gunpowder

The triumphant Ottoman sultan Mehmet II enters Constantinople in 1453, as portrayed by a nineteenth-century French painter.

to launch immense cannonballs. Each night the defenders repaired the walls. By then the population of Constantinople, weakened by disease and lack of food, was probably less than 50,000—far smaller than in the city's glory days. Yet the Byzantines, supported only by a group of Italian soldiers, fought as valiantly as they ever had in their long history.

Finally the Turks decided to attack by both land and water. Because a heavy chain blocked the Golden Horn, they dragged their boats over rocky hills from the Bosporus down into the Golden Horn, behind the chain. After midnight on May 29 the all-out assault began. At last the famous walls were breached. The last emperor, Constantine XI, fought and died with his men. His body was never identified.

For three days the victors pillaged the great city. Then the sultan gave the order to stop, and the Ottomans settled down to establish their own empire, which would last until 1922. The Byzantine Empire was finished.

CHAPTER TWO

THE "HEAVENLY KINGDOM" ON EARTH

The world of Byzantium rested—firmly and fervently—on the Christian religion. Christianity provided the very heart, soul, and muscle of the whole empire.

Christian Belief

The Byzantines believed in the divinity of Jesus Christ—the teacher and prophet who lived in Palestine two thousand years ago and became the center of the Christian religion. They believed him to be the Son of God and the spiritual savior of humankind. They accepted his teachings about God's infinite love and mercy toward humankind, and his commandment to love one another. They looked toward an ultimate Judgment Day when worthy Christians would join Jesus and God in heaven. And they believed that each individual could decide whether to accept these beliefs—or be condemned to hell.

At the core of Christian faith is the doctrine of the Trinity, which states that God exists in three beings: God the Father, God the Son (Jesus), and God the Holy Spirit. According to this belief, Jesus is a form of God, as well as the Son of God. These are difficult ideas to understand, and questions about the nature of Jesus would loom large in religious discussion throughout Byzantine times.

The adoption of Christianity in Byzantium did not happen in a gradual manner. Rather, it was an essential part of the revitalizing of the empire.

Constantine and Christianity

Until the fourth century the official religion of the Roman Empire was

A mosaic of Jesus Christ, holding the New Testament of the Bible, displays stern majesty.

what we call paganism. The Romans worshipped many different gods and goddesses, such as Jupiter, Venus, Apollo, and Mars. In addition, the great variety of peoples included in the Roman Empire all had their own religions. The Roman rulers allowed these cults to continue, requiring only that their subjects submit to imperial authority and not cause trouble.

Unlike many cults that belonged to specific groups of people,

Christianity was an inclusive faith and had widespread appeal, especially for ordinary people and the poor. Its following grew steadily. At times Roman emperors believed Christians might be a threat to the authority of the state, and they ordered cruel persecutions. The Christians, however, were so committed to their faith that they accepted martyrdom and did not weaken.

In 312 Constantine turned to Christianity and persecution ended quickly. According to the story of his conversion, Constantine had a profoundly affecting dream or vision on the eve of a critical battle in his march toward total control of the Roman Empire. He beheld a shining cross and heard the words, "In this sign conquer." Adopting the sign of the Christian cross, he triumphed on the battlefield.

While Constantine's conversion may have actually been a more gradual process, his interest in Christianity went deep. As emperor, he made Christianity legal throughout the empire. He encouraged the teaching of Christianity and had large churches built in Constantinople, Rome, and Jerusalem. Constantinople became not only the seat of a revived Roman Empire and the center of Greek-Roman civilization, but also the most important Christian city. Pagan worship, meanwhile, declined and was finally prohibited throughout the empire in 392.

As it grew, Christianity needed more organization, so a hierarchy of church officials was established. Three of the leading cities in the eastern Mediterranean world—Antioch in Syria, Jerusalem in Palestine, and Alexandria in Egypt—each had a bishop. The patriarch in Constantinople was superior to all the bishops, and the Byzantine emperor was above the patriarch. Usually the emperor and patriarch tried to work together, but when both were strong-minded men, as was often the case, serious conflicts arose.

The Christian Empire

As the state religion, Christianity provided an immensely powerful force for unification. Government and religion were combined in one all-powerful body. Christianity also brought people together in a common faith that they could follow with devotion and enthusiasm. This gave the Byzantines a strong sense of identity, distinctiveness, and destiny.

Christianity was more than just a religion for the Byzantines. It was

Constantine's vision of the cross, which led to his accepting Christianity, as imagined by a fourteenth-century Italian artist

the foundation of their political ideas and systems. When Constantine decided to establish a new capital, he intended it not only to serve political purposes better than the old capital, Rome, but to be a "new Jerusalem," the religious center of the empire as well. Thus Christianity, he hoped, would unify and strengthen the empire and overcome the diversity among its many peoples.

That was not all. The state religion inspired powerful beliefs about

29

the empire itself and the unique role it had to play in the world. According to these beliefs, the Byzantine Empire was nothing less than "heaven on earth." Its mission was to bring about conditions—for the whole world— as close as possible to the reign of God in heaven. While the old Roman Empire had sought to rule by law and military force, the new Roman Empire would unite all humankind under Jesus Christ, the Prince of Peace. This was a mighty mission, but the Byzantines seem to have had complete faith that they could achieve it.

"Correct" Beliefs

The church of the Byzantine Empire is generally called the Orthodox Church. From the start, Byzantium's rulers insisted on an orthodox faith— that is, a universally accepted doctrine or set of beliefs. They believed that anything less than universal acceptance of the "correct view"—the literal meaning of *orthodoxy*—could lead to conflict. This would weaken the church, and hence the state. Indeed, major disputes about religion raged in the early years of the empire.

Between 325 and 787 a series of seven Ecumenical (universal) Councils were held to hammer out differences of opinion and decide on orthodox doctrine. The first and in some ways most important Ecumenical Council was called by Constantine himself, soon after he became the sole emperor. The main concern of this council, held at Nicaea in 325, was the nature of Jesus Christ and his relationship to God, a question that was arousing great controversy. After much debate the church leaders agreed on the doctrine of the Trinity and the doctrine that Jesus had both a divine and a human nature.

Adoption of orthodox views did not end all disagreement, however. Most of the people of Syria, Palestine, and Egypt held to a different view. They insisted that Jesus Christ was wholly divine in nature, a doctrine called Monophysitism (muh-NAH-fuh-sie-tih-zum), meaning "one nature." The church leaders in Constantinople rejected this idea. According to the orthodox view, both the human and divine natures of Jesus were essential to his unique role.

Attempting to stamp out Monophysitism, the Byzantine rulers carried out ruthless persecutions in Syria and Egypt. Many people in those areas grew so angry toward their Byzantine overlords that they were willing to accept the new religion of Islam when it appeared in the seventh century. Religious beliefs therefore played a significant part in Byzantium's losses of territory.

The Emperor's Role

The Byzantines believed that the role of the emperor was all-important in achieving the "heavenly kingdom" on earth. This brings us to one of the most fascinating aspects of Byzantine culture.

In the pagan Roman Empire the emperor had claimed to be divine, one among other pagan deities. Although that notion naturally was abandoned under Christianity, the Byzantine emperor's new role took on even greater importance. He was now the representative of God on earth, a counterpart to Jesus Christ. Each emperor was considered to have been chosen personally by God and was responsible to no one else. Everything

The Council of Nicaea meets in 325 C.E., with Emperor Constantine I prominent among the church dignitaries.

HAGIA SOPHIA

One sight that most visitors to modern-day Istanbul—formerly Constantinople—want to see is the magnificent church of Hagia Sophia. Although often translated as "Saint Sophia," the name does not refer to a particular saint. Rather, it means "Holy Wisdom," referring to Christ.

The first Church of the Holy Wisdom was built by Constantine I on a prominent height in Constantinople. After the church was destroyed in the Nika riots of 532, Emperor Justinian resolved to build a better church to demonstrate the power of the empire. Two architects of rare skill and mathematical ability created a new design, one that would set the pattern for other Byzantine churches. Rather than the traditional basilica, a rectangular building, they started with a square and built a large dome above it. No church of its size or magnificence had ever been attempted before.

The building was completed in five years, in 537. Twenty-one years later the dome collapsed after an earthquake. Undaunted, the architects built an even larger dome. It stands to this day, supported by a rim of windows and delicate small columns that make it look almost as if it is floating on air. Rising 180 feet high and measuring 100 feet in diameter, the dome gives the church an enormous enclosed space. Rare stones from all parts of the empire decorate the interior, and in Byzantine times the whole church glistened with gold, silver, ivory, and above all, lavish mosaics. Thousands of lamps filled the church with light, driving away all shadows.

Hagia Sophia, the heart of Constantinople, embodied the religious faith and worldly pride of Byzantium. As such, it became a special target for invaders. When European knights took the city in 1204, they deliberately desecrated Hagia Sophia. Sultan Mehmet II made a point of ceremoniously entering the church as soon as the city was conquered in 1453. Under the Ottoman Turks, Hagia Sophia became a mosque, its brilliant walls whitewashed. Today, with its mosaics once more revealed, it is a museum—and truly one of the most awe-inspiring buildings in the world.

The magnificent church of Hagia Sophia in Constantinople. The four minarets (towers) were added after the Ottomans conquered Constantinople and turned the church into a mosque.

the emperor did, according to this belief, was based on religion and motivated by religion. Charged with bringing about harmonious order on earth as in heaven, the emperor governed on God's behalf and carried out God's wishes for humankind.

As God's representative, the emperor made a splendid appearance. Everything he did had to follow strict traditions and rituals. Much of his time was spent in grand ceremonies that were designed to display his unique significance and to make an overwhelming impression on everyone who witnessed them. The imperial court was, in fact, meant to mirror God's court in heaven.

A famous example comes from a tenth-century report by an Italian bishop who was given an audience with the emperor at the palace in Constantinople. The visitor first beheld the emperor sitting on a "throne of Solomon"—a golden throne adorned with mechanical birds and lions, with clever devices that made the birds sing and the lions open their mouths, waggle their tongues, and roar. The bishop had been told to expect this, so he just went ahead and got down on the floor, bowing three times as was customary. But when he looked up again, the throne and emperor had disappeared! Looking higher, he discovered that the throne—with the emperor in it, now wearing an even more dazzling robe—had been lifted almost to the ceiling. And there the emperor remained. For the whole time the bishop was in the emperor's presence, he had to tip his head way back, gazing up as though at a heavenly body.

Small wonder that visitors, especially the unsophisticated barbarians, were thunderstruck by the Byzantine court!

The Emperor's Job

The emperor's days were not devoted solely to displays of celestial radiance. He had territory to defend—and extend, if possible. Because the empire was considered to be God's domain on earth, every military campaign had the nature of a holy war. The emperor was therefore a holy warrior, leading campaigns against the infidels (primarily the Muslim Arabs and Turks) and sometimes against intruding Christians from western Europe. Victorious campaigns were celebrated with all the pomp and glory imaginable. Not only did victory mean that the empire was safer for a while, but it was also proof of God's approval.

With all power and responsibility resting in the emperor's hands,

*Byzantine craftspeople were skilled at carving ivory. This panel, measuring about
nine by ten inches, probably represents a triumphant Emperor Justinian I.*

under God's direction, the Byzantine Empire was a highly centralized autocracy. And the sacredness of office was not limited to the emperor alone. Everyone who held public office was working for God, because each individual served the emperor, who represented God. That included a great many people, for the Byzantine government was famous for its large and complicated administration. The emperor himself appointed, dismissed, and kept direct relations with each high official. He did not use an intermediate administrator such as a prime minister, although there was often a person who served as an unofficial "power behind the throne."

A BYZANTINE PLOT

Over the years the word *byzantine*—with a small *b*—has acquired a special meaning. It has nothing to do with the glory of Constantinople. In fact, it's not very complimentary. The word is often used in talking about politics: for instance, a "byzantine scheme." In this sense *byzantine* means devious, roundabout, secretive, two-faced, deceptive.

The Byzantines operated that way much of the time. Although they took pride in their excellent fighting force, they preferred to avoid warfare whenever possible. Sometimes this meant delicate diplomacy, at which they were masters. Sometimes it meant tricking or misleading their enemies, often by making false promises. On occasion they would persuade a threatening enemy that there were richer pickings somewhere else. Frequently they bought off an enemy with lavish amounts of gold, plus fancy titles that didn't mean anything.

Another meaning of *byzantine* is "extremely complicated." This probably refers to the huge bureaucracy of officials who ran the empire. That massive bureaucracy, along with strategies that relied on cleverness and deception, helped the empire survive.

It's an ironic turn of fate that the term *byzantine*—which refers to so much that was admirable—can also have such negative meanings.

From its first days to its very last the Byzantine Empire found unity and strength in religion. At the same time nothing caused more bitter conflict than the religion founded by Jesus, the Prince of Peace. Let us now see what happened when the Byzantines attempted to carry out their ambitious plan to establish God's realm on earth.

CHAPTER THREE

HOW THE "HEAVENLY KINGDOM" WORKED

Iconoclasm

Even with a people united in religion, led by a ruler considered to be God's representative, the path to achieving Christ's reign over all humankind was far from easy. In the eighth and ninth centuries the empire was torn by a religious controversy that affected everyone from the emperor to the simplest washerwoman.

The trouble surged around one central issue: the role of art in worship. Many Christians were devoted to icons—pictures of Jesus, the Virgin Mary (mother of Jesus), and the saints. A question arose: did these images lead to piety and help teach the faith, or did they lead to idolatry—the worship of images—and emphasize too much the human, physical nature of Jesus Christ?

Emperor Leo III (reigned 717–741) took the latter view: that religious images led to idolatry. In 730 he decreed that images of holy figures, including icons and paintings on church walls, should be banned. The policy of iconoclasm (i-KAH-nuh-kla-zum)—literally, "image smashing"—was under way and much religious art was destroyed.

Most of the Byzantine people were dismayed by iconoclasm. Women in particular were upset and angry, because devotion to icons played a vital role in their faith. Monks also vigorously opposed iconoclasm, since monasteries possessed many icons and other religious art.

Waves of iconoclasm rose and fell for more than a hundred years, depending on the views of the reigning emperor and those close to him. The conflict, which led to severe persecution at times, did not end until 842, with the death of Theophilis, the last emperor who promoted iconoclasm. At that point iconoclasm was officially pronounced a heresy,

Angry iconoclasts deface an image of Jesus, apparently at the emperor's order, in this twelfth-century manuscript illustration.

meaning an idea contrary to orthodox belief. Once again, people were free to venerate religious pictures.

East versus West

Orthodoxy triumphed in the Byzantine Empire. What about the rest of Christendom, which was *not* orthodox in faith? Here we come to perhaps the most troublesome problem in the whole history of the empire and its people: the relationship between the Orthodox Church and the Roman Catholic Church.

Although Rome was no longer the seat of even part of the Roman Empire after its fall in 476, it remained the seat of the Catholic Church. Thus there were two centers of Christianity. One was in Rome (the Catholic Church under the pope), and the other was in Constantinople (the Orthodox Church under the patriarch).

In terms of doctrine and beliefs the two branches of Christendom were not far apart. From the start, however, a serious gap developed between the Byzantines and Rome, largely over the question of supremacy.

Many people considered the pope supreme in all Christendom because he had inherited his role from Saint Peter, one of Jesus Christ's apostles, who had founded the first church in Rome. The Byzantines emphatically rejected that view. In their mission to lead humankind to God, they insisted on being their own masters. The patriarch and other officials of the Orthodox Church, they argued, must be independent of the pope's authority. The question of the relationship between pope and patriarch caused a bitter and intense conflict that was never fully resolved.

The conflict between the Eastern and Western churches also reflected a difference in cultures. Eastern Christianity had a Greek character. Greek was the official language of the Byzantine Empire, as decreed by Emperor Heraclius in 627. Both society and religion were influenced by the heritage of classical Greek philosophy and literature. A distinctive Byzantine civilization developed, with language, dress, architecture, ceremony, ways of ruling, and ways of relating to other people all reflecting Greek culture, plus some influence from other Eastern cultures.

Only a few hundred miles to the west in Rome, Latin continued as the language of learning and religion. The Roman Church reflected the cultures of western Europeans, such as the Frankish, Germanic, Spanish, and Celtic

IF YOU LIVED IN BYZANTIUM

If you had been born in Byzantium your way of life would have been determined partly by the facts of your birth—whether you were a boy or a girl, wealthy or poor, free or slave—and partly by your own ambitions and qualities. With this chart you can trace the course your life might have taken early in the tenth century, as a member of a prosperous shipowner's family.

You were born in Constantinople . . . .

As a Boy . . .   As a Girl . . .

You live on a narrow, steep street in the heart of the city, yet in sight of the Golden Horn, where your father's ships are anchored. Your two-story wooden house is attractively decorated with well-made furniture and fine fabrics. An icon of the Virgin Mary, patron saint of the city, stands in a corner, where your family lights candles and worships every evening.

At age 6 you begin attending a good school, where you study classical Greek grammar, reading, writing, and spelling. After a few years you start memorizing the works of the ancient Greek writer Homer. You also study mathematics and some scientific subjects.

At age 15 you continue your schooling at the home of a wealthy and learned man. Although your father would like you to go into his shipping business, you are interested in medicine, and eventually he sees that as a way of social advancement. You learn medical skills from a teaching physician at a hospital.

At age 23 you marry the daughter of an official "on the way up" in the imperial bureaucracy. You and your young wife have a home of your own. Your mother, recently widowed, lives with you and devotes her time to prayer and charitable works.

At age 35 you are respected in your profession as a physician. You do not have as luxurious a life as your parents did, but you are actively helping people, as a Christian should. For your leisure you enjoy strolling in the public forums and gardens, discussing philosophical questions with friends, and writing letters.

At age 6 or 7 you begin your schooling. Your parents, who value education, hire a tutor to teach you and a few girl cousins several times a week. For a few years you get as good schooling as your brothers, but then you must concentrate on housekeeping skills, weaving, and embroidery. You stay mostly at home, although you can watch the street from the secluded balcony that juts out from your house.

At age 15 you are married to a silk merchant's son, who is several years older than you. The marriage is arranged by your parents and grandmother, who negotiate a contract with the other family and provide you with a good dowry. Your property as a married woman is protected by law.

At age 23 you spend your time managing the household and caring for your two children. To help with the household work, you have a young servant and an elderly Bulgar slave.

At age 35 you still spend most of your time at home, rarely going out except to church. Servants do the shopping. You hope that someday women will receive more education and be able to pursue wider interests.

In your old age you are thankful that God gave you a useful, quiet, reasonably prosperous life. At your death you are mourned in a special church service and buried in a cemetery near the church.

peoples, whose traditions were very different from those of the East. The two Christian churches and their people thus were shaped by contrasting cultures. Almost inevitably they regarded one another with suspicion.

A major turning point in the conflict came early in the ninth century. After a long period of disorder in western Europe, a strong Frankish leader known as Charlemagne managed to unite much of that region. In 800 Charlemagne was crowned emperor of the Roman Empire. The ceremony was performed in Rome by the pope, who had political troubles and badly needed the support of a powerful ruler. At that time the ruler in Constantinople was a woman, Empress Irene, and the pope considered a woman ruler to be no ruler at all! He therefore felt free to crown his own emperor, a western European one.

The crowning of Charlemagne was a direct slap at the Byzantines, who considered themselves the rightful rulers of the Roman Empire. Although Charlemagne's empire fell to pieces not long after his death in 814, all popes from then on remained firmly aligned with western Europe.

The Schism

By the middle of the eleventh century the two branches of Christendom had reached a breaking point. The pope and patriarch had been criticizing and denouncing each other for some time. Matters came to a head with a clash between two strong-willed personalities: Patriarch Michael Cerularius and a high church official sent to Constantinople by Pope Leo IX. The two became so angry that each excommunicated the other. This led to a formal break, known as the Schism, in 1054.

The whole Orthodox Church was now completely free of Rome. But the Schism underlay continuing tensions between Constantinople and western Europe, and it led to much future trouble.

Missions and Conversions

Because Christianity has always been a religion intended for all peoples, missionaries have played an important role in church history. The Byzantines sent out missionaries to win converts among Europeans who were still pagan. The Roman Church did likewise, and missions therefore became another area of rivalry.

The Orthodox missions naturally focused on lands within or near the Byzantine Empire, and on peoples with whom the empire had often been in conflict. For example, the Bulgars, one of the empire's greatest adversaries, accepted the Orthodox faith around 870. The empire also gained religious and cultural influence over peoples it did not control, such as the Serbs in the western Balkans.

In the second half of the ninth century two Byzantine missionaries named Cyril and Methodius invented a new alphabet that allowed peoples of eastern Europe to read religious material in their own language. The alphabet, called the Cyrillic, was an important factor in the Russians' acceptance of Orthodox Christianity in 988 and is still used in Russia today.

Meanwhile, Catholic missionaries reached other areas of central and eastern Europe, including Germany, Hungary, Croatia, Poland, and what is now the Czech Republic. With peoples in those lands following the Church of Rome, Europe was divided between the two branches of Christianity.

Lasting Disunity

All hope of reconciliation between Eastern and Western Christendom was destroyed by the Crusades. The pope's declared reason for sending crusaders to Palestine—to rescue the holy city of Jerusalem from the infidel Seljuk Turks—was religious in nature, but that was only part of the story.

The kings and knights of western Europe wanted the fabulous wealth of the East. If they happened to hurt other Christians in their drive for land and gold, that did not bother them. To Western eyes, those "other Christians" were not true Christians at all, because they had broken away from the Church of Rome. They were defiant heretics, no matter how civilized they might be. This attitude reached a peak in 1204, when the crusaders evidently felt no qualms about slaughtering the Christians in Constantinople and desecrating their churches.

Antagonism between the two parts of Christendom could also be seen in the role of the Italian city-states, which were loyal to the Church of Rome. The doge of Venice joined in the plot against Constantinople in 1204, and the merchant cities of Venice, Genoa, and Pisa took advantage of the Byzantines' weakness at every turn.

More than once in the late period of Byzantine history, an emperor tried to bring about unity between the two churches in the hope of winning support from the West against attacking armies. In 1274, when the army of Charles of Anjou threatened Constantinople, Emperor Michael

A fourteenth-century French chronicle depicts the orderly entry of the French and German kings into Constantinople, during the disorderly Second Crusade (1147–1149).

VIII Palaeologus said that he would accept the pope's authority. Later, as the Ottoman Turks drew their noose ever tighter, other emperors also tried this strategy. At the Council of Florence in 1439 Emperor John VIII made a last desperate attempt to gain Western support by accepting certain phrases in the Catholic statement of belief.

Each time, however, the monks and the people of Constantinople would have none of it. They adamantly refused to yield to papal supremacy. The rulers of the West had no interest in shoring up the fast-weakening Byzantine Empire—while the Byzantine people refused union with the Roman Church under any conditions.

The Emperor's Life—and Death

The contrast between the ideal and the reality of the emperor's life is one of the most striking aspects of the whole Byzantine thought system. We have seen that the Byzantine emperor was regarded as God's representative on earth, a counterpart to Jesus Christ. We have glimpsed something of the splendor in which he lived and the reverence his people were supposed to hold for him. But how close did most emperors' careers come to that ideal?

The truth is that not many Byzantine rulers died peacefully in bed. Of the approximately ninety emperors and empresses who reigned between the founding and the final fall of Constantinople, twenty-nine met miserable fates. A number were packed off to exile in monasteries. Some were merely blinded. Others were decapitated, mutilated, bludgeoned, poisoned, stabbed, strangled, and so forth. It would almost seem as though, at times, becoming emperor was like signing one's own death warrant!

How can we reconcile these facts with the image of the divinely protected emperor? Probably the best explanation is a strange twist in Byzantine thinking. The Byzantines apparently reasoned that if a man—or, on rare occasions, a woman—succeeded in gaining the throne, then it was proof that God had chosen that person. It didn't much matter just *how* he had come to the throne. Likewise, if an emperor was murdered or in some other way dispatched, then it was proof that God was finished with him and wanted someone else instead. It was all God's will.

Because of that reasoning, the rules for succession to the throne were never very clearly determined. In Roman times the emperor usually had been selected by the military and by the Senate, a council of wealthy and important men. To some extent, this continued in Byzantine times. Emperors did not even have to be from the ruling classes. Some worked their way up through the military, and some came from modest rural backgrounds. Leadership thus was often based on ability rather than on blood, in principle a good thing.

BASIL BULGAROCTONUS

One Byzantine emperor earned himself the forbidding name of Basil Bulgaroctonus—Basil the Bulgar-killer.

Basil II took the throne in 976, at the age of eighteen. There was nothing elegant or emperor-like about Basil, other than his determination to make the empire great. Short, homely, blunt, dressed in ordinary clothes (and none too clean, it was said), he was unimpressive afoot—but superb on horseback. He learned all he could about both governing and leading an army. An excellent general, he drove his men winter and summer, enduring the hardships alongside them.

Basil's life was one of constant warfare. For the first thirteen years of his rule, he had to deal with contenders who were trying to seize the throne. In Syria he fought the Arabs and recaptured important cities. His main target, however, was the Bulgars. Under a strong king the Bulgars were expanding into a dangerous rival power. They wiped out Basil's army in 986, a defeat for which he determined to have complete revenge.

Slowly but surely, Basil rebuilt his army and carried on his campaign. Finally, in 1014, he got his chance. He defeated the Bulgars, captured possibly as many as 15,000 prisoners—and then sent them back to their king. But every one of those men had been blinded, with each group of 100 led by a man with one eye left. The Bulgar king died at the horrible

Basil II triumphs over the conquered Bulgars, who grovel at his feet. This illustration comes from an eleventh-century Psalter (book of psalms).

sight, the Bulgars' spirit was broken, and their kingdom was soon brought under Byzantine control. Although ruthless in fighting the Bulgars, Basil proved wise and fair in governing them.

Basil died in 1025 at age sixty-seven, while preparing a campaign to retake Sicily from the Arabs. Thanks to him, the empire was larger than it had been since the days of Justinian I, and the imperial treasury was full of gold. But Basil the Bulgar-killer, the ultimate warrior, had never married and left no heir. After his death the empire lacked good leadership and lost ground for more than fifty years.

In practice, however, the throne was often held by hereditary succession, starting as early as Constantine the Great's reign. Ruling families called dynasties clung to power as long as they could, and the office of emperor usually passed from father to son. In general, the Byzantine people seem to have liked it that way: hereditary succession appeared traditional, legal, and proper. At one point in the eleventh century, for example, power fell to a middle-aged woman, Empress Zoë. When her adopted son took over the throne and sent her off to a convent, the populace rioted. "We want our ancestress and mother Zoë!" they shouted in the streets.

Empress Zoë holds a document promising money for the support of the church in this detail from a mosaic in Hagia Sophia.

Usurpers

There were many occasions when someone usurped the throne, seizing power by violence or treachery. And that, too, seems to have worked well for the empire.

Basil I was born in the ninth century on a poor farm in Macedonia, part of the Balkans. A strong and handsome young man, he made his way to Constantinople and eventually got a good job looking after the emperor's horses. The emperor, Michael III (popularly known as Michael the Drunkard), liked Basil well enough to appoint him coemperor. That friendly arrangement did not last long. Within a year Basil had assassinated his benefactor.

Surprisingly, Basil turned out to be an unusually good emperor. He started one of the strongest dynasties, called the Macedonian dynasty. Founded by a usurper, the dynasty was interrupted by four other usurpers and plenty of bloodshed. Members of the ruling family always managed to regain power, however, and the dynasty ruled for nearly two hundred years, from 867 to 1056.

One of the usurpers who intruded into the Macedonian dynasty was

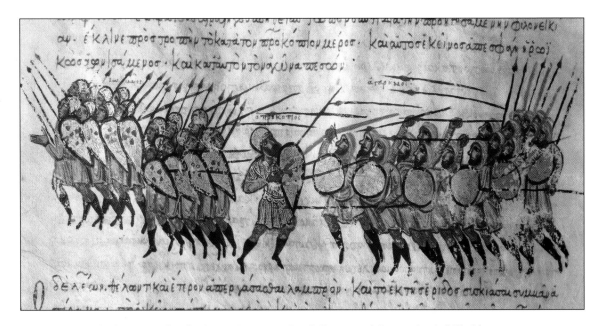

A bad moment for the Byzantine army. Basil I's general Procopius is killed by Arab warriors, as his own soldiers desert in the face of Arab forces.

Nicephorus (nih-SEF-uh-rus) II, a strong general who came to power in 963 after the suspicious death of the existing emperor. Nicephorus in turn was brutally murdered by one of his former military comrades, John Tzimisces (tsih-MIH-seez). John proved to be an outstanding emperor until he died of sickness . . . or poison.

Here are two more examples of the danger that filled the lives of many emperors. In 1183 a usurper named Andronicus I seized power by mob acclaim. After only two years he ended up the victim of mob hatred, tortured to death in public. A particularly shocking case was that of Constantine VI (reigned 780–797). His mother, Empress Irene, ruled in his name while he was young. She evidently loved power so much that she plotted against him for years. Finally Irene got her son out of the way by having him blinded.

Did the Byzantine rulers have a worse record of violence and treachery than the leaders of other societies? That's hard to say. Scholars point out that, despite the many cases of murder and mayhem, the majority of Byzantine emperors were upright men who tried to rule well. And a more important fact must be kept in mind. The Byzantine government worked. Based firmly on the Christian faith, it endured along the same lines, without serious break, for eleven hundred years. Even though beset by attack and weakened from within, it did not break up into many small, squabbling states.

Indeed, it is almost miraculous that the Byzantine Empire survived for so long and, for much of the time, so prosperously. The best clue to its success probably lies in the strength of the distinctive Byzantine culture.

CHAPTER FOUR

LIFE IN BYZANTIUM

Because Christianity underlay the very purpose of the Byzantine state, religion was extremely important in Byzantine society. The Christian community of Byzantium included everyone, regardless of social status, and everyone had a role in expressing the faith.

The Church

Religious sacraments performed at churches—baptism, confirmation, confession, marriage—shaped the Byzantine people's lives. Regular church services took place several times a day. On special days, such as the many festivals and holy days connected with the lives of Jesus and the Virgin Mary, the services reached astonishing splendor. In a setting made as rich as possible, whether a small village chapel or the great churches of Constantinople, the service honored Christ. The prophet whose life had exemplified simplicity was now worshipped as the King of Kings.

The church service, called the Divine Liturgy, re-created the central ideas of the Christian faith. It also reaffirmed that the Byzantine Orthodox state was a holy nation, dedicated to serving God. Each part of the liturgy took a long time, because each had special spiritual and emotional significance. All over the Byzantine Empire the worship service was basically the same. It could be conducted in different languages when necessary, in order to be meaningful to all worshippers. Thus people had a sense of belonging to an eternal and universal faith.

The other side of this picture of unity was that once the orthodox view had been adopted on a vital question, any serious difference was considered heresy and had to be stopped. The Byzantine leaders believed that to create God's kingdom on earth, they had to be absolutely sure of their faith. Ordinary people, too, reasoned that a person had to have the correct faith if he or she expected to go to heaven.

Byzantine artists were famous for their beautiful and vivid frescoes (wall paintings). This eleventh-century fresco from a church in modern-day Turkey tells the biblical story of Judas's betrayal of Jesus.

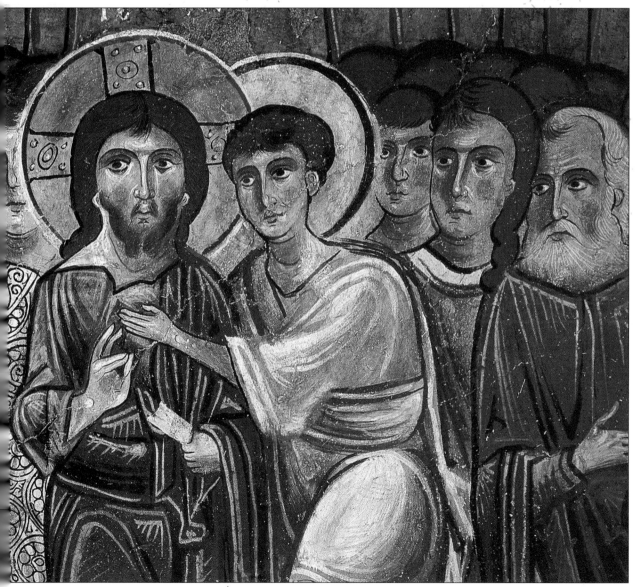

The church of the Holy Apostles in Constantinople, from a twelfth-century manuscript illustration

Yet people evidently loved to talk and debate about questions of faith. Visitors to Constantinople and other Byzantine cities, especially in the early centuries of the empire, observed that everyone was fascinated by religion. From fishmongers to court officials, people talked endlessly about religious ideas and practices. It's surprising that this fondness for discussion and speculation did not produce more breakaway movements. A few groups with ideas different from the orthodox view did appear at various times, yet the Orthodox Church always triumphed—perhaps in part because of the inclusiveness and mystical beauty of the church service.

Monasteries and Convents

Besides numerous churches, the Byzantine religion included many monasteries and convents. These were so numerous and powerful that they were almost like an independent state-within-the-state. When wealthy people wanted to do good works, they established or gave money to a monastery. Thus monasteries became extremely prosperous, controlling a great deal of land "tax free." This weakened the economy of the empire, as the central government could not get income from the lands held by the church.

At the same time, monasteries and convents made valuable contributions to Byzantine society. They provided a refuge for individuals who wanted to escape the problems of the world, as well as for those who were banished for political reasons. Furthermore, much scholarship and writing was carried on in monasteries and convents. In the ages before the invention of printing, the copying of manuscripts by hand was the only way written materials could be preserved and made more widely available. That painstaking task kept many a monk and nun busy.

The Classical Heritage and Education

Remarkably, the Byzantines' devotion to Christianity in no way stifled their respect for their classical heritage, even though that heritage represented the pagan past. They preserved and took great pride in the literature, philosophy, science, and historical

In the sixth century Justinian I founded the monastery of Saint Catherine at the foot of the mountain peak where Moses is said to have encountered God, in the Sinai Peninsula.

writings of the ancient Greeks and Romans. They also admired the statues of pagan gods and goddesses, even though their own religious art was entirely different.

At times it required some hard thinking on the part of Byzantine religious leaders to reconcile the ideas of the pagan Greeks and Romans with Christian thought—but they managed to do it. Byzantine civilization therefore rested securely on the Christian faith combined with the classical intellectual heritage.

The Byzantines took enormous pride in their distinctive civilization. By any standards it was brilliant. Compared with the rougher societies of western Europe and the barbarian hordes, it was absolutely dazzling.

Scholarship and education ranked almost as high as religion in the Byzantines' esteem. Byzantine schools and universities relied heavily on the works of classical writers and philosophers, so that even students preparing for religious careers received a thorough classical education. Young scholars might also receive training from private tutors in the households of wealthy patrons. The university in Constantinople, founded in 425, provided training in the law and humanities.

A large section of the urban male population, including the middle class made up of officials, merchants, and skilled craftspeople, managed

The Byzantines valued learning highly. In this manuscript illustration teachers are lecturing students at one of Constantinople's schools of philosophy.

to get some schooling. Being educated was a source of great prestige. In certain scenic parts of Constantinople, for example, the only individuals allowed to build houses were those who had enough education to "appreciate the view."

Girls, too, might be educated, although not so commonly or so well as boys. Many Byzantine women in the upper levels of society could read and write, were familiar with literature, and had enough education to discuss ideas thoughtfully.

ANNA COMNENA AND THE *ALEXIAD*

Alexius I Comnenus took the throne by force but became one of Byzantium's best emperors. His daughter Anna made that crystal clear in her book about his life, the *Alexiad.*

Anna was a princess *porphyrogenita* ("born in the purple," or from the ruling family). Growing up in the imperial palace, she had an excellent education. At age thirteen she was married to a scholar. He was a good man, but not ambitious enough for Anna.

Unfortunately for Anna's ambitions, Alexius chose her younger brother John as the next emperor. Anna hated her brother. Apparently, so did their mother. After Alexius died, the two women plotted to assassinate John. When caught, they were sent off to separate convents. Anna then devoted herself to writing the history of her father's career. She described in great detail both court life and the endless military campaigns waged by Alexius.

For all his hard work holding the empire together, and despite his popularity with the troops, Alexius was constantly beset by plotting and treachery. Yet, as Anna records, he showed mercy time after time. Her history also describes events such as the First Crusade's passing through Constantinople in 1097. The crusaders were ill-mannered, Anna reports, and they talked too much.

Unlike many emperors, Alexius died in his own bed, surrounded by his devoted family. Anna idolized her father, in spite of his choosing John to succeed him. Although her book is hardly objective, she is considered possibly the first woman to be a serious historian.

Literature

The Byzantines produced an impressive amount of literature, written in Greek. Their great demand for books made scriptoria—the rooms where manuscripts were copied—very busy places.

Although much Byzantine literature was religious, there were also dictionaries, encyclopedias, and books on practical subjects ranging from beekeeping to military science. Poetry was also popular, including love songs and long narrative poems about heroes. One of the most famous Byzantine poets was a woman named Kassia. She is said to have been so beautiful that an emperor nearly made her his wife in 830, but he apparently was discouraged by her superior intelligence and piety. Kassia founded a convent in Constantinople and spent her days writing highly esteemed hymns and wise, brief verses on secular subjects—including the pros and cons of being beautiful.

The Byzantines' respect for their past made them natural historians and chroniclers. They continued the tradition founded by classical Greek and Roman historians such as Herodotus, Thucydides, and Tacitus. A curious thing about Byzantine historians is that they openly plagiarized. Believing that their job was to select and put together material from various sources, they frequently copied other authors' work and saw no need to acknowledge it. In addition to histories, Byzantine scholars left lively, detailed accounts of their own times.

The best-known Byzantine historian was Procopius, who lived at the time of Justinian I and wrote glowing accounts of the emperor's grand buildings and wars. But Procopius seems to have been a bit two-faced. He also wrote a notorious *Secret History* in which he claimed to reveal the emperor's unpleasant dark side—not to mention some astonishing scandals about Justinian's wife, the beautiful and strong-willed Empress Theodora.

Another famous scholar was the eleventh-century historian Michael Psellus (SELL-us). A talented but arrogant educator, Psellus taught at the university in Constantinople, wrote historical works and chronicles, influenced emperors, and played a leading role in political intrigues.

Several emperors, such as Constantine VII "Porphyrogenitus" (reigned 913–959) and Manuel I Comnenus (reigned 1143–1180) also were serious scholars. Some rulers evidently took more interest in their reading and writing than in running the empire.

The beautiful Theodora rose from humble origins to become the empress of Justinian I. This sixth-century mosaic decorates the church of San Vitale, in Ravenna, Italy.

The Rule of Law

Byzantine society placed strong emphasis on the rule of law. One of Justinian I's foremost concerns upon becoming emperor in 527 was to deal with the vast body of laws that the empire had inherited from the Romans. He appointed a well-qualified committee to study and sort out the enormous amounts of material dealing with the law. The organization of the law, called the Code of Justinian, is considered one of the most noteworthy accomplishments of that emperor's long reign.

Justinian also wanted to make the law more humane, in keeping with the ideal of brotherly love taught by Jesus Christ. As a result, the

A servant carries a jug in a mosaic from a large sixth-century Byzantine church discovered in the 1990s in the remote city of Petra, Jordan.

Code of Justinian included new laws that improved the lot of women, slaves, debtors, and other traditionally powerless groups. From then on the theme of protecting the weak and small against the large and powerful would run throughout Byzantine history.

Some Byzantine ideas of mercy, however, sound strange to us today. The death penalty was relatively rare, but when executions were carried out, they often became public spectacles. Many crimes were punishable by mutilation, such as the loss of a hand or the tongue. Blinding was a common punishment, as well as an efficient method for getting a defeated political figure, such as an emperor, out of the way. The Byzantines took seriously the biblical commandment "Thou shalt not kill" and believed that a drastically impaired life was a more merciful fate than death.

Christian charity took more humane forms as well. The idea that Christians should look after one another, caring especially for the poor and weak, appealed to the Byzantines. They supported many hospitals, schools, orphanages, homes for the elderly, and other institutions intended to help the unfortunate. For example, in the twelfth century Emperor John II Comnenus funded a fifty-bed hospital. Well staffed and divided into wards and a surgery, the hospital was many centuries ahead of western European facilities for caring for the ill.

Music

Music is considered one of the finest of the Byzantines' cultural achievements. It had an essential role in church services because the liturgy was sung or chanted, contributing greatly to the emotional effect of the words on the worshippers.

Religious music was performed by the voice only, without accompaniment. The Byzantines had a wide variety of musical instruments, such as horns, lyres and other stringed instruments, flutes, drums, and cymbals, but they considered these appropriate only for secular music. Instrumental music was often frowned upon because it was associated with the theater, banquets, and other forms of popular entertainment.

Composers of choral music wrote down musical notations, using a system of signs that were placed above the words, indicating the notes, rhythm, and accents, and producing complex harmonies. Although none of the Byzantines' secular music remains, much of their religious music has been preserved because the musical tradition has always been kept alive in Orthodox churches. In some parts of eastern Europe Orthodox churches still use original hymns and chants introduced centuries ago by Byzantine missionaries to help win people to their faith.

Art and Architecture: Byzantium's Crowning Glory

Almost all of the Byzantines' secular architecture has vanished, leaving few traces even of the imperial palaces of Constantinople. Fortunately, much religious architecture has survived. Starting with Constantine the Great's plan to make Constantinople the center of Christianity, the Byzantines lavished their wealth and creative talent on their churches.

A typical design for a Byzantine church included a central square space, topped by a large dome. Looking up, worshippers inside the church could feel as though they were standing under the arc of heaven. The impression was enhanced by the beautiful decorations, which covered almost all the wall space and followed a certain plan in churches throughout the empire.

Typically images of the Virgin Mary holding the infant Jesus had a prominent place, while from the greatest height the figure of Christ overlooked all the people in the church. Unlike Western churches, which were dominated by the figure of Christ on the cross, in Orthodox churches Christ often appeared in serene or stern majesty, blessing the faithful. He was Christ the King, ruler of all, rather than the crucified and suffering Jesus.

The Byzantines' most famous form of artistic expression was mosaic work—pictures and designs created from small colored cubes. Elaborate mosaics gleaming with rich colors and gold adorned Byzantine churches. Artists were also skilled at fresco painting—paint applied on a special layer of plaster. Frescoes on church walls and domes displayed

This lively mosaic of the biblical story of the three kings bringing gifts to the newborn Jesus decorates the wall of a church in Ravenna, Italy.

MOSAICS, THE GLORY OF BYZANTIUM

Mosaics are designs or pictures made by fitting together small pieces of stone or similar material. The Romans' elaborate mosaics often represented scenes from pagan mythology, underwater creatures, or bloody fights between men and wild animals. In Roman hands mosaics stayed mostly on the floor. The Byzantines, however, took mosaic art to new heights. They covered the walls and domes of their churches and palaces with spectacularly beautiful mosaics.

The individual pieces from which the mosaics were made are called tesserae. They were cut in small squares measuring about three-eighths of an inch, from thin slabs of stone, colored glass, or ceramic material. The mosaicist spread a layer of plaster on the wall surface, then a second layer of a special, slow-drying plaster. After drawing the design lightly on the plaster, he carefully pressed in the tesserae, one at a time, as close together as possible. By using different colors of tesserae the mosaicist created a picture or design. In some mosaics many different colors of stone were used, creating subtle shading. The garments and faces of the figures look almost as lifelike as in a painting.

Byzantine mosaics are especially striking because of the lavish use of gold. The gold tesserae were made of clear glass with gold leaf— extremely thin sheets of gold—applied on one side or between two thin layers of glass. In the mosaic the glass catches the light with a glistening effect that makes the images, such as figures of saints and kings, seem to hover against a heavenly background.

Although most Byzantine mosaics are in churches, an immense mosaic palace floor has recently been uncovered and restored in Istanbul. Part of Justinian I's sixth-century palace, it is covered with secular scenes: realistic animals, mythological creatures, hunters, trees, children at play, people performing daily tasks.

Byzantine emperors used mosaic artistry to help spread Byzantine culture throughout the empire. Rather than sending ready-made mosaics, they sent the mosaicists to do the work in distant churches and other buildings. In the eighth century Muslim rulers hired Byzantine artists to decorate the Great Mosque of Damascus with colorful mosaics representing trees, rivers, and palaces—still beautiful!

vivid scenes from the Bible, plus images of emperors and empresses and confident Byzantine soldiers.

Besides mosaics and frescoes, the Byzantines were renowned for their icons—pictures of holy persons painted on panels of wood. Icons were kept not only in churches but in people's homes. Relatively small and portable, they could even be carried on journeys. The display of important icons was often a part of ceremonial processions, for instance when armies were setting off for battle or returning victorious.

When we first look at Byzantine art, we may be puzzled. Figures and faces appear to be drawn childishly, even crudely. Had the Byzantines somehow lost the skills of the ancient Greeks and Romans, who portrayed human beings with idealized beauty and physical accuracy?

No, the answer seems to be that the Byzantines wanted to use art in a different way, for their own religious purposes. Instead of showing human beings as they really looked, they wanted to express the idea of holiness and solemnity. To focus on the feeling of eternity rather than the changing conditions of real human beings, they developed a style that

A sixth-century icon of the Virgin Mary and the infant Jesus with two saints is part of the famous collection of icons at the monastery of Saint Catherine in the Sinai Peninsula.

was almost abstract rather than realistic. When emperors and empresses were depicted in mosaics, for example, they were shown wearing their splendid robes, crowns, and jewels, but more as symbols of greatness than as individuals. Similarly, in Byzantine art the Virgin Mary usually looks sad but remote as she holds the infant Christ, without the tender expression often shown in Western paintings.

Relics and Miracles

Devout Christians also revered holy relics—objects believed to be the physical remains of saints and items associated with them, such as bones, splinters from the cross on which Jesus was crucified, and fragments of clothing. Churches kept relics in ornate, beautifully made containers called reliquaries.

The reverence for relics suggests that, despite all their education and respect for classical Greek and Roman thought, the Byzantines had a leaning toward superstition. They believed in omens, dreams, and miracles. They also regarded monks as holy persons with mysterious divine powers, an attitude that helped the monasteries build their wealth and importance.

In the midst of all their worldly glory, the Byzantines must always have been conscious of the threat of danger, whether from demons or from invading barbarians. This probably contributed to a state of constant tension and a desire for supernatural aid. It may also help explain a certain acceptance of cruelty in Byzantine society, in spite of the concern for Christian goodness. The violence with which some emperors—and even patriarchs—came and went, and the occasions of mob fury, are examples.

As it looks to us, the Byzantines' mission of bringing about God's kingdom on earth never had much chance of success. Alienated from the other half of the Christian world, beset by enemies on all sides, they steadily lost territory and wealth until there was nothing left. Yet they persisted stubbornly in their beliefs and pageantry to the end, and the result is a brilliant legacy that we can still appreciate today.

Reliquaries such as this golden treasure dating from the reign of Justinian I were often fashioned in the shape of a cross.

CHAPTER FIVE

GLIMMERS OF THE GOLDEN EMPIRE TODAY

On a sunny day in May 2001, Pope John Paul II visited Athens. This was front-page news, because no Roman Catholic pope had visited Greece—part of the old Byzantine Empire—since before the Schism of 1054. Addressing representatives of the Greek Orthodox Church, the pope said he believed that the Roman Catholic Church should acknowledge wrongs it had committed in the past. He apologized specifically for the crusaders' sack of Constantinople in 1204.

This official apology was accepted by the Orthodox Church leaders—but not by everyone in Greece. Some people still felt such anger over the historic conflict between Constantinople and Rome that they loudly protested against the pope's visit. The Schism of 1054, it appears, is not just "history." Suspicions of the West still run deep among many people who live in countries that were once part of the Byzantine Empire.

Despite the continuing sense of difference, the vital role of the Byzantine Empire in shaping the course of history and culture in both the East and the West is recognized today. Throughout the centuries when European society and culture were in disorder, the Byzantine Empire kept both the Christian religion and intellectual life vigorous. The Byzantines provided a defensive wall against Islam's expansion into Europe, first under the seventh-century Arab Muslims and later under the Turks. This gave European peoples time to develop stronger cultures and states of their own. Without the Byzantines' determination to stand fast, the history and culture of both Europe and the New World would likely have taken very different turns.

These large bronze horses, made in ancient Greece, formerly stood in the Hippodrome of Constantinople and now grace the front of the church of Saint Mark's in Venice.

Religious Heritage

Thanks to their missionaries and the grandeur of the churches and court of Constantinople, the Byzantines spread Christianity throughout much of eastern Europe. Especially significant was the Russians' adoption of Byzantine-style Christianity. The idea of a society uniquely blessed by God, with a semidivine emperor, appealed to the Russians, who became the direct inheritors of Byzantium after the fall of Constantinople. Today, even after generations of neglect and suppression under communist rule, the Orthodox Church of Russia has multitudes of followers.

Similarly, houses of worship all over Greece and large parts of the Balkans, from tiny village chapels to magnificently adorned churches, show the popular devotion to Orthodox

A Byzantine mosaic of the Virgin Mary and Jesus overlooks worshippers in an Orthodox church in modern Russia.

Christianity. In eastern Mediterranean lands such as Lebanon and Jordan, communities of Eastern Orthodox believers keep alive religious beliefs and practices that go back to Byzantine times.

Orthodox monasteries, too, continue in many parts of the Middle East, mostly Greece and Lebanon. Clustered upon Mount Athos, at the tip of a narrow rocky peninsula in the Aegean Sea, are many monasteries where monks preserve religious rituals and traditions of Byzantine origin. In the mountainous desert of the Sinai Peninsula in Egypt stands the monastery of Saint Catherine, founded by Justinian I in a dramatic spot associated with the biblical account of Moses receiving the Ten Commandments from God. The monastery's ancient walls, sixth-century chapel, and famous collection of icons attract numerous visitors.

An Orthodox monastery in Greece, which preserves traces of the Byzantine culture and religious rites, provides a quiet refuge for study and prayer.

Artistic Heritage

In the Balkans, eastern Europe, and Russia, churches and monasteries preserved both the subject matter and style of Byzantine art. For western Europe, on the other hand, Byzantine art was not an end in itself, but served as a sort of stepping-stone in the art history of Western civilization.

During the last two hundred years of the empire, when conditions were desperate and only a few bits of territory were left, Byzantine artists produced some of the finest art of the entire Byzantine period. They influenced painters of the early Renaissance in Italy, where artists and scholars were starting to explore ideas in a new way. Giotto and Simone Martini were two such Italian artists inspired by the Byzantines. Although Italian painters soon moved in different directions, the great flowering of Western art owed its start largely to Byzantine culture.

Several churches in Italy reveal the influence of Byzantium. The eleventh-century Saint Mark's in Venice, one of the world's most famous and magnificent churches, has dazzling mosaics. A platform high over the church's entrance holds four large bronze horses that had stood in the Hippodrome of Constantinople until they were carried off in 1204. Other Italian churches known for their beautiful mosaics, some dating back to the early Byzantine era, can be found in Ravenna, Rome, Palermo, and Milan.

It's not necessary to go to Europe, however, to see churches modeled on the Byzantine architectural plan and decorated with modern mosaic art. Many Greek Orthodox churches in American cities follow these traditions. Music derived from the Byzantine mode also has continuing appeal and is still sung in Orthodox churches and performed by specialized musicians.

Intellectual Heritage

In the empire's last years many Byzantine scholars fled to western Europe, especially to Italy. They brought as much of their libraries as they could, including ancient manuscripts. In that way Europe gained a price-less intellectual heritage, which otherwise might have been scattered or lost.

Byzantine culture served as a bridge in the growth of Western civilization. By preserving the writings of the Greeks and Romans, the

A painting by the early Italian Renaissance artist Simone Martini (1284–1344) reflects the influence of Byzantine art.

A BYZANTINE TOWN FAR FROM CONSTANTINOPLE

Deep in a remote canyon in Jordan stand the spectacular ruins of a city carved from rock. Two thousand years ago, Petra was a wealthy trading center, the capital city of an Arab people called the Nabataeans. It was then taken over by the Roman Empire. But what happened later? Until recently scholars thought that by the sixth century Petra had been abandoned because of earthquakes.

Now we know more about the Petra of early Byzantine times. In 1990 archaeologists discovered a large, splendid Byzantine church, buried in sand. Several other Byzantine churches had been found earlier, but this one is the most impressive by far. The floors are covered with dozens of beautiful stone mosaics depicting animals, birds, fish, human figures symbolizing the seasons, and other designs. The walls and arches apparently were also decorated with mosaics, as many golden glass tesserae (individual pieces used in mosaic work) have been found.

In a room adjoining the church, a large number of papyrus scrolls came to light in 1993. Blackened by a fire long ago and extremely fragile, they can still be read. These documents, which date from 537 to about 594, include wills, contracts, tax bills, and a dispute over a dowry. They show that the wealthy landholding families of Byzantine Petra had to collect taxes for both the empire and the town. These people also helped in the church, monasteries, and hospitals, and some of the men served in the army—there was a Byzantine fortress nearby. Slaves are listed by name, as property. Of the 350 people named, only 27 are women.

By Byzantine times Petra's main source of wealth apparently was no longer trade but agriculture, carried on outside the canyon. The beautifully decorated church and the documents prove that Petra was not abandoned by the sixth century, but continued for many more years as a prosperous city in the Byzantine Empire.

The floor of a large sixth-century Byzantine church in the ruins of Petra, Jordan, is covered with intricate mosaics like this one.

Byzantines connected the classical culture with the intellectual life of the Renaissance, and eventually with the modern world.

The riches that the Byzantines bequeathed to the world through their art, literature, architecture, and music more than offset the negative images of political treachery and violence that they also left behind. Their story, with all its turbulence, did not end in 1453. The brilliant culture they maintained for more than a thousand years has made a profoundly valuable contribution to civilization today.

The Byzantine Empire: A Chronology

B.C.E.

c. 658   Byzantium founded by Greek colonists

C.E.

293	Diocletian reorganizes Roman Empire
306	Constantine I becomes coemperor
312	Constantine accepts Christianity
324	Constantine reunites Roman Empire under his sole command, chooses Byzantium as new capital
325	First Ecumenical Council, held at Nicaea, defines Orthodox Christian faith
330	Byzantium, now called Constantinople, inaugurated as new capital of Roman Empire
392	Pagan religions prohibited, temples closed
413–439	Theodosius II builds immense city walls
476	Rome falls to Ostrogoths; end of western part of Roman Empire
527–565	Reign of Emperor Justinian I
529	Code of Justinian compiled
532	Nika riots in Constantinople
533–540	General Belisarius reconquers North Africa from Vandals, and Sicily and Italy from Ostrogoths
537	New Church of the Holy Wisdom—Hagia Sophia—completed in Constantinople
610–641	Reign of Heraclius
627	Heraclius defeats Persians
632	Death of the prophet Muhammad in Arabia; religion of Islam starts to expand
636–646	Arab Muslims take Palestine, Syria, Persian Empire, Egypt
674–678	First siege of Constantinople by Arab Muslims
711	Arab Muslims complete conquest of North Africa and much of Spain
717–718	Second siege of Constantinople by Arab Muslims
717–741	Reign of Leo III, first iconoclast emperor
726–842	Period of iconoclasm (interrupted from 780 to 813)

751	Lombards take Ravenna; end of Byzantine rule in northern Italy
800	Charlemagne crowned Roman emperor in the West
842	Icon veneration restored after death of last iconoclast emperor, Theophilis
867–886	Reign of Basil I, founder of Macedonian dynasty (867–1056)
870	Bulgars convert to Orthodox Christianity
976–1025	Reign of Basil II "Bulgaroctonus"
988	Russians convert to Orthodox Christianity
1018	Basil II completes conquest of Bulgars
1054	The Schism: final break with Church of Rome
1055	Seljuk Turks take over Baghdad
1071	Seljuk Turks defeat Byzantine army in Anatolia; Normans take southern Italy
1081–1118	Reign of Alexius I Comnenus
1082	Major trading concessions granted to Venetians
1098	Crusaders stop at Constantinople and then take Jerusalem
1118–1143	Reign of John II Comnenus, son of Alexius I
1187	Muslim leader Saladin defeats crusaders and retakes Jerusalem
1202–1204	Fourth Crusade: crusaders capture and sack Constantinople
1204–1261	Latin emperors rule in Constantinople
1261	Michael VIII Palaeologus, emperor of Nicaea, takes Constantinople from Latins, restores Byzantine rule
1266	Charles of Anjou threatens Byzantium; defeated in Sicily in 1282
1290–1337	Ottoman Turks advance through Asia Minor
1402	Turks defeated by Timur and Mongols at Ankara; respite for Byzantines
1439	Council of Florence: last attempt to achieve unity between Roman Catholic and Greek Orthodox churches
1448	Constantine XI becomes emperor
1453	Constantinople falls to Ottoman Turks, led by Mehmet II; end of Byzantine Empire

GLOSSARY

autocracy: a government ruled by one person with unlimited power

barbarian: to the Byzantines, a foreigner, and specifically someone not Greek or Roman—thus considered not civilized

bureaucracy: a body of many government officials of different ranks who work by fixed rules

Christendom: the part of the world in which Christianity prevails

chronicler: an account of recent events, written in the order in which they occurred

Crusades: a series of "holy wars" between the eleventh and thirteenth centuries, waged by European Christians to recapture Jerusalem and other formerly Christian cities from Muslim control

desecrate: to deliberately destroy, damage, or insult a sacred place or object

ecumenical: universal, representing everyone in the Christian Church

excommunicate: to formally deprive a person of membership in the church

forum: an open space in a city used as a marketplace or for public assemblies

heresy: a belief or an opinion contrary to the established religious beliefs and judged not acceptable

hierarchy: the group of clergy and officials who govern a church, ranked in order of importance and power

humanities: the branches of learning concerned with human thought and creativity, such as philosophy, literature, languages, and art

iconoclasm: the destruction or prohibition of icons; literally, "image smashing"

infidel: someone who believes in a religion other than one's own; to Byzantine Christians, anyone who was not a Christian

liturgy: the prescribed ceremonial acts and words used for public worship in a church

monastery: a place where monks—male members of a religious community—live and work together, separate from secular society. The counterpart for women is a convent.

Monophysitism: the belief that Jesus Christ had only one nature, divine, as opposed to the belief that he was both divine and human

orthodoxy: the religious views considered correct and approved, excluding differing views

pagan: a person who believes in many deities, rather than in the one supreme God of the Jewish, Christian, and Islamic faiths

porphyrogenitus: a term applied to a child born to a ruling monarch; literally, "born in the purple," referring to a special room in the palace decorated with rare purple stone

schism: the division of a group into opposing parts

secular: worldly, not religious

succession: the arrangement or order by which a new ruler succeeds, or follows, the previous ruler

venerate: to profoundly revere; veneration is the expression of deep respect for something regarded as sacred

FOR FURTHER READING

Nonfiction

Asimov, Isaac. *Constantinople: The Forgotten Empire*. Boston: Houghton Mifflin, 1970.

Chubb, Thomas Caldecot. *The Byzantines*. Cleveland: World Publishing Company, 1959.

Downey, Glanville. *Constantinople in the Age of Justinian*. Norman, OK: University of Oklahoma Press, 1960.

Hearsey, John E. N. *City of Constantine, 324–1453*. London: John Murray, 1963.

Lemerle, Paul. *A History of Byzantium*. New York: Walker and Company, 1964.

Norwich, John Julius. *A Short History of Byzantium*. New York: Vintage Books, 1999.

Sherrard, Philip. *Byzantium*. New York: Time-Life Books, 1966.

Treadgold, Warren. *A Concise History of Byzantium*. New York: Palgrave, 2001.

Whitting, Philip, ed. *Byzantium: An Introduction*. New York: New York University Press, 1971.

Fiction

Barrett, Tracy. *Anna of Byzantium*. New York: Delacorte, 1999.

Dickinson, Peter. *The Dancing Bear*. Boston: Little Brown, 1973.

ON-LINE INFORMATION*

"Byzantine Art and Architecture" at
> *http://vandyck.anu.edu.au/introduction/byz/artserve.html*
> Visual examples of Byzantine architecture and art.

"Byzantine Studies on the Internet" at
> *http://www.fordham.edu/halsall/Byzantium*
> A general introduction to Byzantium and guide to Byzantine studies.

"Byzantium" at *http://www.byzantium1200.org/*
> Intriguing computer reconstructions of many buildings in Constantinople as they may have looked around the year 1200.

"The Glory of Byzantium" at
> *http://www.metmuseum.org/explore/Byzantium/byz_1.html*
> The Metropolitan Museum of Art's introduction to Byzantine history and its collection of Byzantine objects.

"Hellenic Ministry of Culture, Odysseus" at
> *http://www.culture.gr/*
> Click on "Museums, Monuments, and Archaeological Sites," then on "list of museums" for the Byzantine Museum of Athens and some smaller collections.

"Internet Medieval Sourcebook" at
> *http://www.fordham.edu/halsall/sbook1c.html*
> Interesting selection of actual sources from Byzantine writing—historical, government, religious, and so on.

*Websites change from time to time. For additional on-line information, check with the media specialist at your local library.

BIBLIOGRAPHY

ACOR Newsletter. American Center of Oriental Research. Amman, Jordan.

Angold, Michael. *The Byzantine Empire, 1025–1204: A Political History.* London: Longman, 1984.

Buckler, Georgina. *Anna Comnena: A Study.* London: Oxford University Press, 1929.

"Byzantine Cultures, East and West." *Athena Review* 3, no. 1 (2001).

Comnena, Anna. *The Alexiad of Anna Comnena.* Translated by E. R. A. Sewter. Baltimore: Penguin Books, 1969.

Diehl, Charles. *History of the Byzantine Empire.* Translated by George B. Ives. New York: G. E. Stechert, 1945.

Garland, Lynda. *Byzantine Empresses: Women and Power in Byzantium, AD 527–1204.* London: Routledge, 1999.

Maalouf, Amin. *The Crusades through Arab Eyes.* New York: Schocken, 1984.

Mathews, Thomas F. *Byzantium: From Antiquity to the Renaissance.* New York: Harry N. Abrams, 1998.

New Catholic Encyclopedia. Washington, D.C.: Catholic University of America, 1989.

Oxford Dictionary of Byzantium. 3 vols. New York: Oxford University Press, 1991.

Procopius. *The Anecdota, or Secret History.* Cambridge, MA: Harvard University Press, 1954.

———. *History of the Wars.* Translated by H. B. Dewing. New York: G. P. Putnam's Sons, 1924.

Talbot, Alice-Mary, ed. *Byzantine Defenders of Images: Eight Saints' Lives in English Translation.* Washington, D.C.: Dumbarton Oaks Research Library and Collection, 1998.

Treadgold, Warren. *The Byzantine Revival, 780–842.* Stanford: Stanford University Press, 1988.

Tripolitis, Antonia, ed. and trans. *Kassia: The Legend, the Woman, and Her Work.* New York: Garland Publishing, 1992.

Ware, Timothy. *The Orthodox Church.* London: Penguin Books, 1997.

INDEX

Page numbers for illustrations are in boldface

ABOUT THE AUTHOR

"My first visit to Istanbul in my student days left only a 'pleasant-enough' impression, but while working on this book, I went to see Constantine's capital again—and was enthralled by the reminders of Byzantium's glory. The grandeur of Hagia Sophia, the mosaics of Chora Church, the stately pillars of the cistern, even the gloomy halls of the rarely visited palace dungeon . . . all were quite thrilling."

Elsa Marston has written both fiction and nonfiction about the Middle East and North Africa, including *The Ancient Egyptians* and *The Phoenicians* in the CULTURES OF THE PAST series, a biography of the prophet Muhammad, *Women in the Middle East: Tradition and Change,* and a new novel set in ancient Egypt, *The Ugly Goddess.* She finds the Byzantines, who are relatively little-known although very much "present" in the Middle East, particularly fascinating because of the way Byzantine history sheds light on other aspects of that region's past. Elsa lives in Bloomington, Indiana, with her husband, Iliya Harik, professor emeritus at Indiana University; they have three grown sons. She enjoys tennis, hiking, music, and yearly trips to the American West and the Mediterranean East.